Machines at Work
Fighter Jets

by Allan Morey

Bullfrog Books

Ideas for Parents and Teachers

Bullfrog Books let children practice reading informational text at the earliest reading levels. Repetition, familiar words, and photo labels support early readers.

Before Reading

- Discuss the cover photo. What does it tell them?
- Look at the picture glossary together. Read and discuss the words.

Read the Book

- "Walk" through the book and look at the photos. Let the child ask questions. Point out the photo labels.
- Read the book to the child, or have him or her read independently.

After Reading

- Prompt the child to think more. Ask: Have you ever seen a jet in the sky? Do you think it was a fighter jet? Would you want to fly a fighter jet?

Bullfrog Books are published by Jump!
5357 Penn Avenue South
Minneapolis, MN 55419
www.jumplibrary.com

Library of Congress Cataloging-in-Publication Data

Morey, Allan, author.
  Fighter jets / by Allan Morey.
      pages cm — (Machines at work)
  Summary: "This photo-illustrated book for early readers describes fighter jets and the parts that help them fly fast and hit targets in battle" — Provided by publisher.
  Includes bibliographical references and index.
  Audience: Ages 5-8.
  Audience: Grades K-3.
  ISBN 978-1-62031-107-3 (hardcover) —
  ISBN 978-1-62496-170-0 (ebook)
  1. Jet fighter planes — Juvenile literature. I. Title.
II. Series: Bullfrog books. Machines at work.
UG1242.F5M665 2014
623.74'64—dc23
                                      2013049158

Series Editor: Wendy Dieker
Series Designer: Ellen Huber
Book Designer: Anna Peterson
Photo Researcher: Kurtis Kinneman

Photo Credits: George Hall/Corbis, 23bl; Photri Images/Alamy, 16–17, 23tr; Stocktrek Images/Stocktrek Images/Corbis, 20–21; Welshi23/Dreamstime.com, 8–9; Defense Imagery/TSgt Michael R. Holzworth, 12–13; Ed Darack/Science Faction/SuperStock, 11; Gary Neil Corbett/SuperStock, 17 (inset); iStock/GrLb71, 3; iStock/rusm, 1; iStock/the _ guitar _ mann, 22; Shutterstock/Frontpage, 6–7; Shutterstock/Gwoeii, 24; Shutterstock/Ivan Cholakov, 4, 5, 18 (inset); Shutterstock/mholka, 14–15; Shutterstock/mobil11, cover; Shutterstock/Sergey _ Bogomyako, 10, 23br; Shutterstock/skaljac, 14 (inset); StockTrek Images/SuperStock, 18–19, 23tl

Printed in the United States of America at Corporate Graphics, in North Mankato, Minnesota.
3-2014
10 9 8 7 6 5 4 3 2 1

Table of Contents

Fighter Jets in the Sky

Look! Up in the sky!

It is a fighter jet.

It is used in war.

Zoom!

The jet is fast.

It has two jet engines.

jet
engines

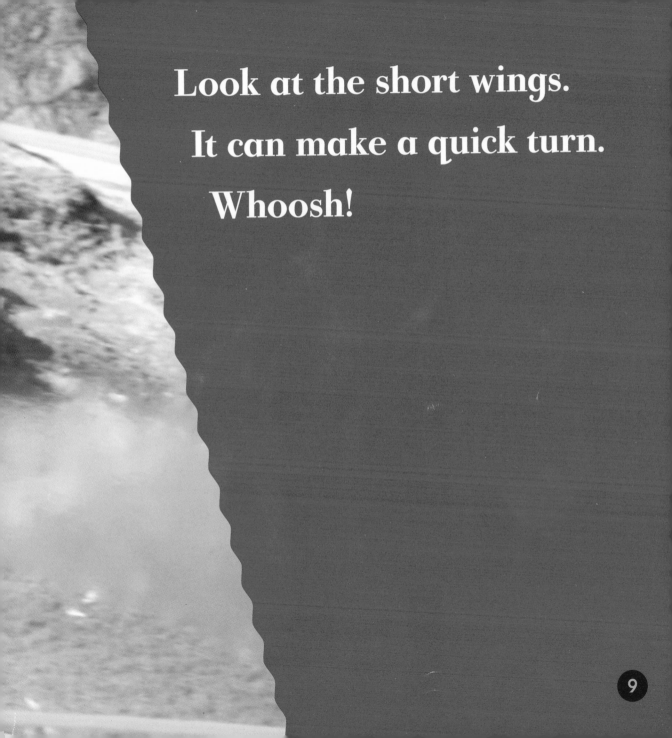

Look at the short wings.
It can make a quick turn.
Whoosh!

Bob is a pilot.

pilot

RESCUE →

1. PUSH BUTTON TO OPEN DOOR
2. PULL RING OUT 6 FEET TO
   JETTISON CANOPY

DANGER
EJECTION
SEAT

DO NOT PAINT

88-0401

He flies the jet.

HUD

Do you see the window?

It has a HUD.

H is for Head.

U is for Up.

D is for Display.

Bob looks at the HUD.
He sees a target.

target

HUD

15

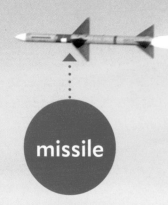

missile

Ready. Aim. Fire!
Bob shoots a missile.
It hits an enemy plane.

17

Bombs are in the plane.

A door opens.

They fall to the ground.

Boom! Boom!

bomb door

bomb

19

Fighter jets fly
in a group.

They keep the
sky safe.

Parts of a Fighter Jet

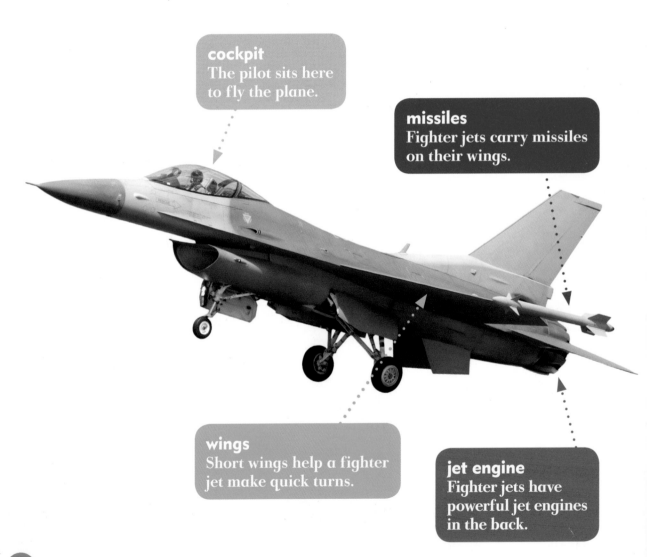

cockpit
The pilot sits here to fly the plane.

missiles
Fighter jets carry missiles on their wings.

wings
Short wings help a fighter jet make quick turns.

jet engine
Fighter jets have powerful jet engines in the back.

Picture Glossary

bomb
A weapon used to hit a target on the ground.

missile
A weapon that flies through the air to hit targets in the sky.

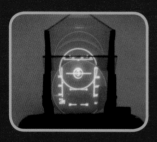
HUD
Head-Up Display; it shows information on the window so pilots can look up while flying.

pilot
A person who flies an airplane.

Index

To Learn More

Learning more is as easy as 1, 2, 3.

1) Go to www.factsurfer.com

2) Enter "fighter jet" into the search box.

3) Click the "Surf" button to see a list of websites.

With factsurfer.com, finding more information is just a click away.